JUST THE JOB

The Employment and Training of Young School Leavers

A Summary Report

G J Pollock and V M Nicholson

Hodder and Stoughton
for
The Scottish Council for Research in Education

SCRE Publication 74

ISBN 0 340 26713 5 (Cased)
     0 340 26715 1 (Limp)

Printed and bound in Great Britain for Hodder & Stoughton Educational, a division of Hodder & Stoughton Ltd, Mill Road, Dunton Green, Sevenoaks, Kent, by Lindsay & Co Ltd, 16 Orwell Terrace, Edinburgh EH11 2EU.

CONTENTS

ACKNOWLEDGMENTS

I should like to express my thanks to all those who have contributed at various stages to the completion of this research study:

to Training Services Division of MSC and the European Social Fund for the financial support which made the work possible;

to Miss Frances Nolan who worked as Research Officer on the project for 17 months and was responsible for the preparation of the interview schedule;

to the interviewers and the young people themselves for their co-operation;

to Mrs Sheenagh Rochow and Mrs Ethna Charleson for their valuable assistance in the coding of the information collected and their diligence in dealing with various problems that arose in the course of the study;

to Mrs Rosemary Wake for her work in preparing and editing this summary report from the much larger report presented to TSD in 1978;

to Miss Elizabeth Moffat, Miss Linda Stark, Mrs May Young, and Mrs Sheila Milne for their patience in deciphering my hieroglyphics and typing the manuscript.

In particular my special thanks are due to my co-author Miss Valerie Nicholson, Research Assistant, who joined the project at a late stage and was responsible for much of the analysis and the initial writing up of the data.

G J POLLOCK

December 1980

The report of which this is a summary was presented to the Training Services Division of the Manpower Services Commission in October 1979, under the title 'From School Into Work'. The Appendix lists the tables in that full report, which is available at the Scottish Council for Research in Education, price on application.

CHAPTER 1

THE BACKGROUND TO THE STUDY

Are young people leaving school to enter the workforce adequately prepared for what lies ahead? How far do the hopes and expectations they held while still at school match up to their actual experiences in seeking, and settling into, jobs and further training? Such matters are the concern not only of the individual but also of employers and all those involved in the provision of effective careers guidance and training. In 1976 the Training Services Agency (now the Training Services Division) of the Manpower Services Unit agreed to support a research study on the employment and training of young school leavers in Scotland. This is a summary of the resultant report which was presented to the TSA in October 1979, under the title 'From School Into Work'. The full report, including the tabulated data, is available at the Scottish Council for Research in Education.*

Aims of the Project

The Employment and Training Project had three main aims: firstly, to investigate how pre-employment aspirations and expectations match with real-life experiences in applying for, being accepted for, and training for jobs; secondly, to compare the employment and training opportunities available to young people of both sexes in various areas of Scotland; and finally, to assess the initial impact of the 1975 legislation relating to female employment and training opportunities. The extent to which the researchers were able to fulfil these objectives is examined later in the report.

The aims were set in accordance with those in the first 5-year plan of the Training Services Agency, who supported the project. This plan had identified young entrants to the workforce as a priority group of special national importance and also indicated that many had had "only limited preparation for the transition from full-time education to the world of work". This limited preparation was seen as possibly leading to a situation in which young people may have unrealistic aspirations and expectations concerning employment and training, and consequently, as affecting their future ideas and attitudes towards remaining in the jobs they enter or the training they receive.

---

* Price on application to SCRE, 15 St John Street, Edinburgh, EH8 8JR.

In the same 5-year plan, attention was drawn to the position of women in the workforce, and to their concentration in specific types of occupation, in spite of the widening aspirations of women at work. New legislation had been introduced in 1975 in order to ensure that women and girls were offered more opportunities in employment and training. It was therefore possible that the effects of the Equal Opportunities Act might begin to show among new school leavers, with girls beginning to enter traditionally male spheres of occupation and industrial training.

The Employment and Training project per se was carried out between August 1976 and April 1978, but it had developed as an offshoot of a larger longitudinal study, begun in 1974, called 'Trends in Secondary Education' which itself grew from a follow-up of pupils who had participated as 10-year-olds in an international study of achievements in science and reading comprehension*.

The Trends in Secondary Education Project

Since 1974 a study has been continuing on the effects of changes in the organisation of secondary education in relation to pupils' measured attitudes, interests and achievements. This was done by carrying out a longitudinal follow-up of a random national sample of some 2,000 Scottish pupils involved in the 1970 international survey. Thus the 1970 data constituted the base-line for the Trends programme. The data included, in addition to scores on science and reading tests, details of home background, father's occupation, sex, VRQ, and scores for interest in science, liking for school and motivation. In 1974 this same sample of pupils, now aged 14, were traced to their secondary schools, and followed up through the remainder of their secondary education and into first employment and/or further or higher education. A second set of test scores in reading and science was obtained together with further measures of interest in science, liking for school and motivation. Central to the Employment and Training Project, details of job and educational aspirations were also collected.

In 1975 the extent of the awareness of post-school educational opportunities among the sample was investigated by means of a

---

* The details of this investigation were reported in 1973 in *Science in 19 Countries* by L C Comber and John P Keeves, and *Reading Comprehension in 15 Countries* by R L Thorndike (John Wiley & Sons, New York, and Almqvist & Wiksell, Stockholm).

semi-structured interview carried out on an individual basis in the school situation. Information was collected on reasons for leaving school; satisfaction with school courses and curricula; actual or expected occupational choice; expected study in further or higher education and awareness of possibilities for such study; and finally, to a limited extent, the career and vocational guidance provided by the home, the school and the careers service.

From 1975, as the sample members completed their period of compulsory education, schooling, examination results, choice of job and entry to further or higher education were also recorded. Among the topics investigated were: how early leaving relates to earlier attitudes and motivation; the stability of the vocational choices of students expressed at the age of 14; the relationship of attitudes and motivation at primary level; how an increasingly comprehensive system of education affects staying-on rates, and how the gifted and less able pupils fare in such a system vis-à-vis the former selective system; the relationship between specialisation in science and earlier interests and achievement in this field; the extent to which pupils find themselves constrained by choices made in second year of secondary school and the implications for later educational and job aspirations.

The follow-up of the young people while still at school was supported financially by the Social Science Research Council and the Scottish Education Department.

Members of the sample were free to leave school from 1975 onwards, and in 1976 the Training Services Agency agreed to fund an extension of the programme to enable a study to be made of the employment experiences of those young people in the sample who had left school by June 1976. The main results of that study are presented here in this abbreviated version of the full report.

CHAPTER 2

THE SAMPLE AND THE DESIGN
OF THE PROJECT

Design of the Project

The *Trends in Secondary Education* cohort originally studied in
1970 was selected on a two-stage basis. A random national sample
of 105 primary schools was selected with probability proportional
to size, and then, within the selected schools, pupils were chosen
with an inverse probability, using date of birth as the basis for
random selection. The sample of pupils so chosen (N = 2183) was
checked against known national statistics and its representa-
tiveness verified.

The sample of young people chosen to participate in the
Employment and Training survey was defined as all those
members of the Trends in Secondary Education cohort who had (a)
been interviewed at school at age 15+, (b) left school by June
1976 and (c) opted for employment rather than continued full-
time study in the further education or higher education sectors.

This gave an initial total of 855 young people to be interviewed
and provided a random national sample of young school leavers.

The data on the employment and training of the young people
were collected by means of a personal interview normally
conducted in their own homes. The interview took approximately
one hour and was based on a semi-structured schedule. It was
also planned to collect data from the employers of the young
people. One in three of the employers was asked to complete a short
postal questionnaire, giving a brief description of the firm, and
indicating its size and the type of training which it gave young
workers. Each firm was asked to indicate whether it was prepared
to discuss the employment and training of young workers more
fully with the research team. On the basis of this information, it
was hoped to select some 50 heads of training sections for in-
depth interviews, within which it would be possible to probe more
fully into the training process. The data from the employers was
intended also to serve as a means of checking on the reliability of
at least some of the information provided by the young people in
their interviews.

Difficulties Encountered in Data Collection and Field Work

The interviews were planned to be carried out in the period
from February to July 1977, approximately 12 to 15 months after

4

the young people had left school, some in June 1975, and others at Christmas 1975 or in June 1976.

Delays in reaching agreement with interested parties over the contents of the interview schedules meant that full scale field work could not begin until April 1977. This left three months rather than five to undertake the 855 interviews, since many of the young people were unavailable in July, this being the holiday month for Scotland. Such a task, despite the recruitment of extra interviews, was not physically possible, and the problems increased when two of the seven part-time interviewers dropped out and could not be replaced. As a result, few interviews were carried out in Highland Region, and parts of Strathclyde were not covered.

There were also various losses from the sample, due to factors such as emigration, refusal to be interviewed, and removal to unknown addresses. The interviewers actually made 539 contacts, but these resulted in only 400 interviews. Of the 316 *not* contacted, 59 were in Highland Region, 47 in Ayrshire, 68 in Lanarkshire and 40 in Renfrewshire. Had it been possible to adhere to the original schedule of five months, almost all members of the original sample could have been contacted.

The response rate to the employers' questionnaire was disappointingly low. Of the 191 questionnaires issued, only 68 (36%) were returned and only 37 firms were prepared to be interviewed further. This poor response made it impossible to regard the returns as in any way representative, and, although some in-depth interviews had been conducted, it was reluctantly decided that it would not be profitable to proceed further in this area of the project.

However, it was possible to check the employers' returns received against the statements made by the young people employed by them, and the two sets of data corresponded very well. On the basis of the restricted evidence available from employers, it would appear that the comments made by the young people are generally valid and that, as a group, they present a reliable picture of young people's reactions to their employment and training.

Representativeness and Significance

Although the sample actually interviewed was not geo-graphically representative, nevertheless when it was checked against the original total sample of 855 no significant differences in terms of characteristic data obtained from earlier stages of the

Trends in Secondary Education programme were found. For example, no differences were found in terms of measured attainments, socio-economic status or occupational aspirations.

It is legitimate therefore to regard the group of 400 interviewees as representative of the original 855, and, as such, despite the overall deficiencies in geographical terms, the results can with reasonable confidence be generalised to Scotland as a whole. Because of the large number of comparisons to be made, a nominal 1% level of significance was set as the basic criterion for claiming statistically significant differences.

In fact, as none of the comparisons by area achieved this level of signficance, no significant differences between areas are reported anywhere in the text. The employment and training opportunities available to the young people in the areas studied did not differ sufficiently to warrant special mention. However, it should be borne in mind that some areas of Scotland, e.g. Highland Region, were not studied.

There are significant sex differences, particularly in the types of jobs sought and aspired to and in terms of training experience. These have been clearly outlined in the text where they apply.

CHAPTER 3

ATTITUDES TO SCHOOLING

Liking for School

This section is concerned with the young people's attitudes to school, both before and after leaving. Of the whole group, while still attending school, 73% were keen to leave as soon as possible; 21% had no strong feelings about leaving school, and only 6% expressed reluctance to leave, most because they liked school, but a few because they wished to gain further qualifications.

It should be borne in mind, however, that the bulk of the group under study consisted of early leavers, i.e. pupils who left school at the first leaving date after reaching the age of 16, and that they represented only approximately half of the total age-group. The remainder who stayed on at school were keen to stay on and gain further qualifications, as other survey data have shown.

In retrospect, 45% of the young people in the study were sure that they had left school at the right time. 23% wished that they had left school sooner, while 16% regretted that they had not stayed longer before leaving. The remainder (17%) felt unable to commit themselves as to whether it would have been better to leave school at a different time.

72% of the 62 young people who later wished that they *had* remained longer at school gave as the reason that they would have liked to have gained more qualifications. This change of mind may be a reflection of their experiences in trying to find employment and, possibly, finding they had insufficient qualifications to compete with others in the job market. This supposition is supported by the fact that a further 19% of the sub-group indicated there were no jobs available, and therefore wished they had stayed on longer.

The reasons given for the earlier attitudes to school were varied. Of the whole group many complained about school and were keen to leave because they disliked it (39%), or felt that staying on was a waste of time since they were not sitting 'O' or 'H' grade examinations (9%). Others were more positive in their opinions, 19% preferring to be at work rather than at school, and 4% wishing to earn money and be independent. 10% considered that they had enough education, and were satisfied with the qualifications they already had.

That most of the young people involved in the study were

7

anxious to leave school, and happy that they left when they did, is further confirmed by the fact that 81% of the whole group indicated they enjoyed work more than school. The young people were very positive in the reasons they gave in support of their opinions. 30% of this sub-group considered they enjoyed more freedom and independence, while 17% enjoyed earning money, and said that they liked work more than school because they 'got paid for it'. Others enjoyed the content of work more than their school work, 14% finding it more interesting and varied, and 6% believing that they were learning a lot more than they did at school. A further 10% gave 'meeting more people' as their reason for preferring work to school.

Usefulness of Curriculum

This section is concerned with whether, after leaving school, the young people found any of the subjects they had done at school useful in their work. Whether they required to hold any qualifications in these subjects is not relevant here, but is discussed in the next part of this chapter.

The young people were asked what subjects, if any, they had found useful in their work, and why. They were also asked if there were any subjects that they now regretted not having taken at school, and if so, what these were, why they did not take them at the time and why they now wished they had. In all cases the young people were allowed to name up to three subjects and were asked to give their reasons, for each subject named, separately. In presenting the results we have combined the data for subjects together.

41% of the group indicated that they had never found any of the subjects they had studied at school to be of any use at all at work. Overall, for this group of pupils, there existed a feeling that their school work was irrelevant to the type of work in which they were involved. There was also a criticism implied, that school had not sufficiently prepared them for work. Of the remaining 59%, a considerable number (27%) specified one school subject only, slightly less (21%) specified two subjects, and only 11% specified three or more, as useful at work.

Not surprisingly, essential or 'basic' subjects were frequently indicated as being the ones found most useful; for 22% of the whole group, English; for 18%, arithmetic; and for 12%, mathematics. The frequency of secretarial subjects (11%) obviously arises because many girls take up clerical and typing jobs. Technical subjects of various kinds were also mentioned frequently (17%), mainly in terms of woodwork, metalwork and technical drawing, and again these subjects have obvious vocational connotations. The science subjects, and in particular physics (5%), were mentioned by some 10% of the group.

When asked why they found these subjects useful, many (66%) indicated that the subject material was used a lot in their job, or that knowledge of the subject helped them to do the job.

However, 65% of the whole group had no suggestions to make as to what additional subjects they would like to have taken at school. Only 1 in 3 expressed any regrets about not taking a particular subject and most of those named only one subject, a few named two, and only five specified three subjects. On balance, therefore, most of the group were reasonably happy with the curriculum followed. The alternatives suggested were generally vocationally orientated or practical subjects, which, it was thought, would have been more useful for work and might have helped them get either a job, or a better job. Nonetheless 15% did think that the subject might be interesting or enjoyable. When asked why they had not taken these subjects, 59% of this sub-group (21% of the whole group) blamed the school, either because the option system had required them to make a choice they now regretted, or because school resources had not provided sufficient places for those wanting to take particular subjects. The remaining 41% (15% of the whole group) believed they them-selves had made a wrong decision, failing to realise at the time how useful the subject would prove to be.

Importance of Qualifications

The young people studied in the survey were drawn largely from the lower half of the ability range. Their qualifications, in terms of formal school examination passes, were very varied. 47% of the group did not have any 'O' grade passes at all, and 21% had only one or two passes, but 16% had more than five passes. In terms of individual subjects, only in English and arithmetic were appreciable pass rates (one in three) obtained. However one in four of the group had passes in both of these subjects. Secretarial subjects and mathematics were the only other subjects passed by more than 7% of the group.

Only 7% of the group had gained further academic quali-fications since leaving school: generally they had attained 'O' grade passes in English or arithmetic, although a variety of other subjects had also been taken.

64% of the group thought qualifications were important in

getting jobs, mostly because they felt qualifications influenced employers and gave people a better chance of getting good jobs. The remainder placed little or no importance at all on qualifications. A curious contradiction emerged between the numbers who in general terms, thought qualifications were important, and the numbers who had actually been required to possess particular qualifications for their present job.

77% of those in employment said that they had not needed any specific qualifications for their job. For those who had (22% of the subgroup), English, arithmetic or mathematics were the subjects most often specified, and most of them required two or more 'O' grade passes. It would seem from the information provided that although specific qualifications may not be regarded as pre-requisites for certain jobs, employers may, nevertheless, use them as a screening device for short-listing applicants for further consideration, after which qualifications have no further importance.

Only 35% of the group felt that, with different qualifications, they might have secured a better job. Within the sub-group there were typically significant sex differences in the types of jobs involved. More boys than girls (39% v 3%) thought they could have got into a trade; more girls than boys (44% v 18%) thought they could have got a routine white-collar job. Generally, for boys, a better job implied a skilled job in engineering or building, or, in the non-manual field, a clerical job; for girls it implied clerical work, secretarial work, or nursing. These figures again emphasise how traditional outlooks affect the types of job both boys and girls aspire to, as well as the ones they actually do get.

Preparation For Work

Different aspects of preparation for leaving school and finding a job were examined, and young people were asked their opinions on the kind of preparation they received, eg careers guidance, work experience schemes and link courses at technical colleges.

The provision of careers advice is obviously a major aspect of preparation for work and for leaving school. Indeed, it is such a major topic that the whole area of guidance is discussed in detail in Chapter 4, and, apart from the references that arise directly from the young people's general comments on preparation for work, the topic is not discussed further here.

Just over half the young people (51%) considered that they had been provided with insufficient help in preparation for leaving school and finding work. When asked why they thought this, most of the dissatisfied group (N = 204) were very condemnatory of possible sources of help. 72% said they were never told anything, and a further 12% that they had only seen the Careers Officer once, and they didn't get much help from him. An additional 10% blamed the school guidance system, saying that they seldom either saw the careers teacher or were given careers talks, and that help was given only to the clever children who were staying on at school or going on to higher education.

For this sub-group of young people the indictment of the careers guidance given before leaving school is indeed severe and raises questions about the efficiency of the service provided.

The dissatisfied group were asked to expand their comments further by indicating the ways in which the school might have helped them more. The main suggestions made included being given more advice about jobs, or being told about the difficulties in finding work (27%), the provision of a specific careers teacher to give more help generally, the provision of more talks from firms' representatives and more visits to firms (12%) and more advice on how to apply for jobs (13%). It is clear that almost all the suggestions relate to additional careers advice.

On the other hand, 43% (N = 171) of the whole group were equally positive that they had received sufficient help and preparation for work. The reasons quoted in support were equally revealing. The Careers Service, both within and outside the school, was widely praised. 43% of the satisfied group indicated that the school gave careers talks (30%), that a careers/guidance teacher was available to help (9%) and the careers library proved informative (4%). The Careers Officer was mentioned by 36% of the satisfied group again in terms of talks and films (14%), help at interviews (18%) and with fixing up a job (3%).

The school and/or teachers also figured prominently for 15% of the satisfied group as sources of help in finding work, and arranging interviews for jobs. Other lesser aspects of the role played by the school, which were seen as helpful by the satisfied group, included the provision of work experience (2%) and technical college visits or courses (3%).

Comparisons of the satisfied and dissatisfied groups present a major conflict of opinion and raise difficulties about interpreting the true state of affairs in schools, particularly as regards careers advice and guidance. On the one hand, almost 4 out of 5 of the satisfied group praised the careers guidance provided for them and found it helpful. On the other hand, the dissatisfied group generally attacked the careers guidance provided through either the school or the careers service, and in very severe terms. Since both groups constitute approximately half of the total sample, and are spread all over schools, the evidence is very contradictory. Clearly the schools are providing a careers guidance service, but why it is effective with many and equally ineffective with many others has still to be resolved.

The whole area of careers advice and guidance is returned to in Chapter 4.

Work Experience

Only 40 (10%) of the sample had been offered work experience while still at school, and, of these, 7 indicated that they themselves had not been willing to accept the opportunity. Thus, only 33 (8%) actually experienced this type of work preparation.

The young people involved underwent a variety of different opportunities in work experience — five worked in a local factory, three in a shop, six in a hospital or playgroup. Others did unskilled manual work as a labourer or worked in parks.

Most of those involved enjoyed their work experience, but only half were sure that it had been of benefit to them. 11 definitely found little benefit in their work experience and 5 could not make up their minds. In general, those who found it beneficial did so for the insight it gave into various jobs, and for the experience it gave of the work situation.

Those who found work experience of no benefit usually said this was because (a) they they didn't particularly want to do it in the first place or (b) because it hadn't done them any good and wasn't like real work. This latter group were perceptive enough to realise that they would be treated differently as workers than as school pupils.

Although 1 in 3 of those who had actually done work experience were not convinced that it had been of benefit to them, 70% of the young people who had not had the opportunity for work experience would like to have done it. 18% indicated that they definitely would not have wished to do it, a figure which is comparable with the refusal rate of those offered the opportunity of work experience at school.

When those who would have liked to go on a work experience scheme were asked why, 50% gave the same reason as those who actually found work experience beneficial, ie they thought it would have given them experience of the work situation and an insight into different jobs. Other reasons put forward were that it might have helped them to make up their minds about what job to do (11%), or to find out something about the type of job they were actually going to do (8%).

The remainder offered a variety of reasons. 13% were optimistic that it might have helped them find work after they had left school, since an employer is more likely to employ an inexperienced person whom he knows will be an industrious worker, than someone for whom he can only rely on references. Another 10% thought work experience would have been better than wasting time at school, or that they would have found it interesting and enjoyed it.

The small group (N = 67) who did not want to do work experience were very sceptical about its merits. 16 thought that it would have been of no benefit to them and would have been no help in the work that they were going to do. 15 already knew what they wanted to do anyway and so did not consider work experience would have helped them, while another 13 were adamant that they didn't want to do it at all. Of the remainder, 5 indicated that they were too busy at school to do work experience; 4 that they did not want to work in the places available; and 3 that they didn't want to do work experience because they were not paid for it.

Use of Technical College Resources

Visits

33 (8% of the sample) indicated that the school had arranged for them to visit a Technical College. Only 28 had actually gone on the visit, since 5 indicated that they were not willing to accept the chance offered. The vast majority (92%) had not been offered a visit to a Technical College at all.

For most, the visit to a Technical College had lasted one day or less and no visit had lasted longer than 4 days. Many (21) had found their short visit interesting, and only 3 were prepared to say their visit was not interesting. Of those who found their visit interesting, 10 did so because of work that was going on there, particularly in computing. 8 were interested in seeing what the college and its courses were like, while 3 saw it as a change from school. The 3 who had found the visit uninteresting said this was because they had been unable to do what they had wanted to do.

49% of the young people who had not been offered a visit to

Technical College said that they would have liked to go. A further 11% were undecided, but 40% were definite that they would not have wanted to visit a Technical College.

Courses

82 young people (21% of the sample) had been offered the possibility of a course at Technical College by the school, more than for any other form of help or preparation of work discussed so far, and 7% actually undertook such a course. One of the effects of ROSLA has been to lead schools to reconsider the curriculum they offer to the less bright or non-certificate child during his/her last year at school. Increasingly, more and more schools are making use of the resources available in Technical Colleges, to provide what they see as meaningful experiences for young people prior to entry to work.

The courses the young people had taken at College were mostly vocationally orientated. 15 had taken a course in engineering and 12 a course for a specific trade. Other courses commonly pursued were secretarial courses (11), catering courses (9) and hairdressing (5). 12 had also taken a mixed general course covering a number of trades.

As might have been expected, there were significant differences in the types of courses taken by boys and girls. Boys were more likely to follow an engineering course, specific trade courses, or the mixed general course, whereas girls were more likely to follow a secretarial, catering or hairdressing course.

Generally, technical college courses were provided either on the basis of one or two days a week for a specific period of time, or in continuous blocks of one or more weeks. For over half of the group who had taken courses (53%), the period at college lasted, in aggregate, three weeks or less, and approximately 1 in 4 had attended for only one day a week for six weeks. Only 3 people had the opportunity to attend for more than one term, and these were young people taking a one-year course in catering or secretarial studies on a full-time basis.

56% of the young people involved considered the courses beneficial, but 36% were equally convinced that the courses they took at college were of no benefit to them.

Those who found their course beneficial, generally did so because it had taught them a lot. 13 indicated that that they had learned about different aspects of work in their course, while a further 9 thought that they had learned more at college than they had at school, and that in some cases the college course had helped them to pass examinations. 8 others had enjoyed their course and found it of general interest and a further 3 indicated that attending college had helped them decide what job they were going to do after leaving school.

Of the 26 who had not enjoyed their time spent at college, 20 stated this was because they found the course they took not relevant to the job they wanted to do in the future or the course they wanted to follow at Technical College later.

As in the case of visits to Technical Colleges, a substantial number (46%) of the young people who hadn't the opportunity to take a course at Technical College while still at school, would have liked to do so (N = 306), but again a large proportion (40%) had definitely no wish to take such a course.

Of those who would have liked to take a course at Technical College many (39%) thought it would have helped them to achieve their aspirations either in getting a job, or a better job, or might have helped them to reach a decision on the most suitable job choice. Others (26%) were interested in particular college courses, and 14% saw the course as an opportunity to find out what Technical Colleges were like. The remainder had more cynical attitudes, 11% indicating that anything would have been better than doing nothing at school and 4% that they might have learnt more at college.

Of the people who had no desire to take a college course, even had it been offered (N = 108), 36% indicated that this was because they were not keen on further training. A further 26% said that a course would have been of no help since no courses relevant to them or their future job were available.

Others indicated a liking for school as their reason for not wanting to go to college. 13 (12% of the sub-group) preferred being at school and another 7 (7%) were more interested in obtaining their 'O' Grade and Higher qualifications at school than in attending college. A further 9 indicated that they already knew what they wanted to do and preferred to go straight to work.

It seems clear that many young people would have welcomed the opportunity to have undergone schemes like work experience or link courses at Technical College, and, on the evidence available, many would have found them beneficial. However, the resources to provide these opportunities are still not readily available, and so only a small percentage of an age-group are able to participate.

Careers Guidance

As the provision of careers advice is a major aspect of preparation for leaving school and entering the work force, this is dealt with in detail in the next chapter.

CHAPTER 4

ADVICE ON EMPLOYMENT

Sources of Guidance before Leaving School

It is clear that many young people desired help and advice in deciding what their career should be. Although much of this advice was formally provided by the Careers Services, family influences also played a large part in determining the final careers choice of the young people.

Careers Service

A disturbingly large proportion of the group (45%) considered they had not received any careers help at all while at school, in spite of the fact that 86% of the group had had at least one interview with the Careers Officer before leaving school. Those who recognised they had received careers help were divided almost equally in opinion between family (particularly parents) and the Careers Service (both within and outwith school), as to which had been the greatest source of help (29% v 23% respectively).

In general, parental advice tended to be more job-specific than the advice offered by the Careers Service, as might be expected.

Only 1 in 3 of the whole group had been given specific recommendations on jobs, mainly from members of their family. Of the 134 who had received job-specific advice (from any source), most of the boys (75%) had been advised to get a skilled job or trade. Many of the girls had been advised to get jobs as clerks or typists (34%) or nurses (16%), although shopwork (12%) and factory work (12%) were also popular. Only 4% had been advised to go into further education on a full-time basis. There was a tendency for advisers to encourage aspirations to a higher level than was attainable in practice. 42% had been advised to go for a skilled trade, yet only 29% of the group attained one. 14% were advised to go for a higher non-manual post but only 9% got one. Again the advisers generally suggested that the young people look for good working conditions and security in their job (46%), but others (27%) had suggested specifically that the job concerned would be an appropriate one for the person concerned.

Practically everyone in the group had been interviewed at least once by a Careers Officer (86%), indeed 15% had been interviewed at least three times, but many found the interview(s) of little help (55%). Only 1 in 3 of the group (31%) found the interviews positively helpful, and this generally because they had proved very informative. Those who found them unhelpful did so for two main reasons: firstly, that the Careers Officer had not offered any advice at all (20% of the whole group); and secondly that he had not found them a job (10% of the whole group), although there were other more specific complaints. The data indicate a conflict between the role the Careers Service sees for itself and its role as seen by the young school leaver. The Careers Officer generally sees his role as one which is basically *informative*, whereas the young school leaver wants the Careers Officer to be more *directive*. There is a need to ensure that young people are made aware of the more limited role the Careers Service has to play, so that false hopes are not raised with consequent disillusionment and complaint when these hopes do not come to fruition.

Despite all the advice available, 31% of the group were still unclear about the work they wanted at the time they actually left school. Again this indicates a need for the Careers Service to consider how to make itself more effective, so as to reduce this figure to a more acceptable level.

Of those who had decided what they wanted to do (69% of the group), boys generally were looking for a skilled trade in engineering (32%), building (19%) or motor and garages (14%), and girls for jobs as clerks and typists (40%) and in nursing (22%).

Approximately 59% of this sub-group were actually able to get the job they desired, although 1 in 12 of these had already changed to another job by the time of the interview. Of those who had been unable to get the job they desired, many (40%) found the jobs were just not available, and 20% found they had insufficient qualifications. This is clearly a reflection of a current very competitive job situation facing young school leavers, where, with *many* seeking *few* jobs, qualifications can play an important part in the initial selection procedure.

Sources of Guidance After Leaving School

On leaving school many people were still unclear as to the kind of job they were seeking, and a considerable number of those who had their minds made up were unable to get the job they wanted. Thus people still had a need for guidance and help with employment even after leaving school.

Official Agencies

Just over half of the group (57%) had received some additional help or advice in finding employment from one or more official agencies like the Careers Service, the Employment Offices and Job Centres. Many of the sub-group (43% of the whole group) had kept in touch with the Careers Service while 27% had visited the local Employment Office. The fact that few (15%) had visited a Job Centre is hardly surprising since Job Centres were still developing in Scotland at the time of the interviews and many areas did not have one in operation.

The Careers Service recommendations made to the young people after they left school were narrower than those made before they left. Jobs in typing or engineering were seldom suggested, presumably because most vacancies were now filled. In terms of skill-levels, it was the unskilled and routine non-manual jobs which were recommended rather than the skilled manual and higher non-manual jobs aspired to prior to leaving school.

1 in 3 of those who visited the Careers Office after leaving school (56 out of 167) were still dissatisfied with the help given, because they had not been found a definite job. The false conception that some young people have of the role of the Careers Service, referred to earlier, again emerged.

Most people who visited the Employment Offices did so merely to register. Few (1 in 3) claimed to have found help and advice here.

In the case of those who visited the Job Centres, 25 of the 44 who responded claimed to have been given little or no help, half of them saying that they had merely been left to look around and that no help was offered.

Overall, 40% of those who had approached the official agencies after leaving school thought that more could have been done for them, but, when asked to specify how, it was clear that their responses were coloured by the difficult job situation generally facing the unemployed. What they basically wanted was to find a job, or to have more choice in terms of job vacancies. Advice was considered helpful by 38% of the sub-group, and unhelpful by 57%. It is clear that many based their judgment of helpfulness on whether the advice was effective in producing a job, rather than on the intrinsic quality of the advice.

Other Sources of Advice

The young people were also asked to indicate what help or advice they had received from other than the official agencies. Only 17% (N = 57) had had such advice, which was almost entirely from their family and friends. The advice given had usually helped the young person to get a job, or had told him about a job that was available, or at least gave encouragement to continue seeking employment. Most of the small group concerned regarded the advice as helpful because it was constructive and often resulted in employment, and also, perhaps, because it came from family sources.

To sum up, then, just over half of the group felt that they had received insufficient help in preparing for leaving school and finding work, in particular making severe criticisms of the careers advice they had received both at school and from the external careers service.

CHAPTER 5

LOOKING FOR WORK

Number and Types of Job Sought

This section is concerned with the number and types of jobs for which young school leavers *applied*. Whether or not the young people actually *obtained* employment in any of these jobs is not relevant here.

The majority of young people (73%) had started looking for jobs before they left school. Of those who had (N = 291), very few (2%) had started more than 6 months before leaving school, and most (58%) had waited until 2 months or less before the leaving date, before starting to seek employment.

Of the minority (N = 105) who did not start looking for work until after they had left school, 45% started immediately they left, and 74% were out of school for a month or less before they started to look for work. 13% explained that they had not started looking for work before they left school because they did not need to, in many cases because they knew that they already had a job secured, for example in a family business, or were intending to take a full-time course at a college before seeking work. Despite this early start in looking for work, most young people did not find work quickly, over half of them taking 2 months or more to find a job, although most had obtained employment within 6 months. Only 7% took longer than 6 months and 2% were still unemployed at the time of the interview, having been unable to find any kind of work since leaving school.

However, if taken at face value, these figures may be misleading. Many of these young people, as we will see later, were first employed in temporary jobs (eg Job Creation), or in jobs which they themselves regarded as temporary stop-gaps. Many accepted jobs which were not the kind of work they wanted in the long term, but which (they felt) were better than being unemployed. This is supported by the fact that more young people (8%) were unemployed at the time of interview, having been initially employed, and that some others had a rapid turn-over of jobs, often because of dissatisfaction with their first jobs.

Most had to make numerous applications for jobs before finding employment. Only 29% were successful with their first application, the remainder requiring to make numerous applications (21% had to make more than 10 applications) before being successful. The information supplied by the young people certainly does not indicate any reluctance on the part of school leavers to look for work, nor does it support the criticisms sometimes levelled at them of laziness or indifference to employment. It does however reflect the shortage of posts available and, possibly, a reluctance on the part of employers to employ people who who have had no experience of working.

Did They Aim Too High?

One possibility, of course, is that the young people may have been over-ambitious in the types of jobs they initially sought. About 1 in 10 of the young people was successful in finding higher level non-manual jobs involving some form of supervisory role. However the number of young school leavers who can hope to take up initial employment at these higher levels is obviously limited, since a predetermined level of academic qualification is generally essential for entry.

The majority of the boys (55%) took up a skilled manual trade, whereas the girls generally took up routine non-manual jobs (64%), and, to a lesser extent, semi-skilled manual jobs (20%). The industries which the young people entered upon on first taking up employment were widely distributed and varied. As expected, strong sex differences emerged. The most popular areas for girls were clerical work (22%), shop work (17%), typing etc (11%), textile factories (9%), and other factories (10%). For boys, the most popular areas were engineering (20%), building trades (16%), and agriculture and farming etc (9%). In interpreting these figures it should be borne in mind that young people in Highland Region were not interviewed.

A comparison with the skill level of the applications made in seeking jobs indicates that for girls there is little difference in overall pattern. The main differences between jobs sought and first employment lie in the areas of clerical work and hairdressing. 32% of girls sought clerical jobs, but only 22% obtained one. On the other hand only 1% sought hairdressing initially but eventually 5% took up employment in that area.

For boys, however, the differences in pattern are much clearer. There has been a distinct shift in skill level, particularly in the case of manual occupations. It appears that many boys who initially hoped to get a skilled trade had to lower their sights and eventually accept either a semi-skilled or unskilled post. In the early applications 66% of boys applied for skilled jobs but finally only 55% found one. Initially only 9% of boys sought semi-skilled or unskilled jobs, but eventually 25% accepted one. In terms of the industries considered the main changes lie in engineering, the nationalised industries, factory work and agriculture. 26% sought a job as an engineer but only 20% gained one, whereas initially only 4% sought factory work, but 9% took up employment there. Again, 6% sought employment in the nationalised industries like Gas, Coal and Electricity, but only 2% were successful. On the other hand, initially only 1% sought employment in agriculture, but 9% had their first job in this area. (Again, note that Highland Region was not included in the survey.)

Comparisons of all the applications made for jobs indicated that girls, as a group, were generally able to obtain the kind of job they wanted both in terms of skill-level and industry — the possible exception being clerical work. For boys, however, the situation was different, particularly so in the case of the manual occupations. Approximately 10% of boys were unable to get the skilled manual job they sought, usually in engineering, and had to settle for semi-skilled or unskilled work in factories or in agriculture. Initially only 9% of boys sought semi-skilled or unskilled jobs but eventually 25% accepted one. Few members of the group were given an element of choice — indeed only one 1 in 6 was actually offered more than one job. The majority of the group were, for the most part, happy to accept the first job offered them.

There was little evidence of widespread assessment procedures in the selection of individuals for jobs. Just under half the group (47%) received interviews in connection with their applications, but only 10% received any form of written test, and fewer still (5%), a practical test. Boys were much more likely than girls to receive a written test, usually in connection with selection for an apprenticeship.

Difficulties Encountered in Seeking Employment

When the difficulties that these young people met in seeking employment are reviewed, a far from pessimistic picture emerges. Most (93%) had been offered at least one of the jobs for which they had applied, and 43% had been offered the first job for which they had applied. (This latter figure appears to contradict a previous figure — the explanation lies in the fact that many members of the group submitted a number of applications at the same time, one of which was successful and so they responded as being successful in their first application.) Nevertheless many had had to make numerous applications before being successful. A small proportion (9%) had not accepted jobs they had been offered, usually because those jobs did not involve the sort of work they were looking for, or because the working conditions or pay were not satisfactory.

Those who were fortunate enough to have had a choice of jobs (15%), generally used the criteria of better working conditions and better pay in reaching their final decision.

Only 2 members of the group had turned down all the jobs they had been offered and were still looking for employment, 1 in catering, the other in engineering. Both had taken further courses in order to improve their qualifications, thereby deferring entry to employment to a later date.

Approximately half of the sample (49%) said they had found it difficult to get a job. The majority of this group (58%) attributed this either to the scarcity of jobs or to the fact that too many people were applying for jobs. A further 16% ascribed it to their lack of the necessary qualifications or experience, while 12% said that there were no suitable jobs available.

Those who had not met with difficulties in finding a job were those who had been given the first job they had applied for, or thought they had been lucky in having applied at the right time. Others felt that the fact that they had attained the necessary qualifications had simplified the task of finding a job, and others still, had had advantages in that they had worked in the job previously, on a part-time basis, or had contacts there through family or friends.

CHAPTER 6

ATTITUDES TO WORK

Previous Job History

In this section we are concerned with the period between the young people's leaving school and their entering on their state of employment or unemployment at the time of the interview. It does not cover the types of job applied for but deals with the previous jobs people had been employed in, and the periods of unemployment they had experienced, during that time.

Understandably, considering the economic situation, many of the young people (58%) had been unemployed for varying periods of time between leaving school and starting work. Most of the group, however, had been able to take up employment either directly after leaving school (42%) or within the next two months (43%). Only 4% had remained unemployed for more than 6 months. It was notable that 58% of the whole group were still working in their first job at the time of the interviews. However, a considerable number had changed jobs since first starting work, and this had not always been of their own choice.

On the whole, those who had changed jobs had tended to be working in unskilled manual and routine non-manual jobs. Few changes had been made by those in skilled manual or higher manual jobs. The changes also tended to be made by those working in particular occupations — shops, catering and hairdressing. Very few indeed took place in engineering.

Those who had changed jobs also tended to be in less well paid jobs. Most had earned £20 or less per week compared with an average of £23 for the whole group.

Most of those who had changed from their original job gave not particularly positive reasons for having accepted it in the first place. Over half of this sub-group felt that they had been given little option but to accept the job: it had been the only one available at the time (17%); it had been the first one offered (13%); or because they had just wanted to be employed (14%). A further 8% saw their first jobs as temporary stop gaps where they had no intention of staying permanently. Only 36% had positively chosen to accept their first job as a desirable one to have.

When asked the reasons why they had given up these previous jobs, the young people concerned fell into three main groups: roughly one-third had been sacked or made redundant, one-third had been dissatisfied with certain aspects of the work or conditions, and one-third had left to take up what they saw as a better position elsewhere — one offering better pay, an apprenticeship or more favourable prospects.

In addition to the 35 young people who were unemployed at the time of the interview, another 49 members of the group had been unemployed for one or more periods since first gaining employment. This latter sub-group was largely made up of those who found difficulty in holding onto a job for any length of time, and who seem likely to have similar difficulties in the future.

The Employed

365 (91%) of the sample were employed at the time they were interviewed and, of these, 249 were in their first job. Almost all the group were employed on on a permanent basis, but 4 were working part-time and 14 (4%) on a temporary basis, mainly on Job Creation or Community Industry Schemes established to relieve unemployment.

Finding the Job

48% had got their jobs through their own efforts by applying directly to the firms concerned, or by answering an advertisement, or because they had worked with the same firm on a temporary basis before. Most had, however, received some help from other parties, mainly parents and family (18%) and the Careers Service (24%). 1 in 4 had felt they had had to accept their present job because it was either the only job or the first job they had been offered, and they wanted to be employed. However, some had managed to realise their ambitions (14%) and others had obtained jobs that they found interesting and/or skilful (17%).

As regards the firm they worked for, 44% specified no particular preference, but others did. Some had joined a family business or worked beside relatives (7%), others chose their firm for reasons such as security and good pay or good working conditions (28%).

Settling in

83% of the young people had had at least some idea of the type of work they would be asked to do, before they started. In general, information had been provided by members of the supervisory staff, either at management level (31%), supervisor level (20%), or by personnel staff (15%). 4%, however, had been told about the job by a member of the training staff, and relatives and friends (16%) had also played a part. On actually starting work, most advice and information had come, not unexpectedly, from within the firm itself. On the first day the 3 main sources of information were managers or bosses (21%), supervisors or foremen (36%) and other established workers (28%). Thereafter, the pattern changed, and most of the subsequent information was provided through an established worker (44%), and to a lesser extent by the immediate supervisor or foreman (26%). Almost all the young people (88%) felt that they had been told enough about the job by their various sources of information, and very few specific omissions were reported.

Just over half of the employed young people (51%) were working beside relatives or friends and had found this beneficial, as knowing what to expect at work and having someone to turn to for advice on problems, etc, they had been able to settle in better. Indeed, 1 in 3 attributed their getting the job in the first place to the fact that a relative or friend worked there.

Many lived very near their workplace, 66% taking less than 20 minutes to reach their firm. Only 3% faced a journey longer than an hour.

As regards the young people's attitudes to their present jobs, the general picture was very much one of satisfaction. 85% were happy with their jobs and many planned to remain with their firms either permanently (61%) or for at least a few more years (13%). The group emphasised that they found their work interesting and enjoyable (41%) and their workmates congenial (19%).

Approximately 1 in 4 of the group were hoping to change their jobs. Many of this dissatisfied group were still anxious to get jobs in what tend to be popular and hence fairly competitive areas such as engineering, clerical work, and nursing. A few were planning to join the forces.

The Unemployed

8.8% of the whole group were unemployed at the time of the interview, a total of 35 young people (13 boys and 22 girls), but only 11 of this unemployed group had never had a job since leaving school. Of these 11, 5 had taken courses of full-time study or training for part of the time since leaving school but had still not yet succeeded in getting a job. It should also be borne in mind that 10 members of the whole group were involved at the

c

time of the interviews in Job Creation or Community Industry type schemes for varying lengths of time, and were temporarily off the unemployment register. 26 members of the currently unemployed group had been unemployed for less than 6 months, and of these 8 had been so for a month or less. 9 were long term unemployed (more than 9 months), including 3 for more than a year. Most of the young people were still seeking the skilled or non-manual jobs to which they had aspired originally, only 1 in 3 having lowered his or her sights and being willing to accept any job just to be employed.

Only 12 members of this unemployed group thought that lack of necessary qualifications had led to their failure to find a job, most of those believing that they needed more 'O' grade passes. 4 had considered returning to school to gain further qualifications; others (12) had considered going to college to gain additional qualifications — 9 in vocationally oriented courses such as catering, secretarial work and nursing and 3 in SCE subjects. 13 members of the unemployed group had already undergone some additional training which they had believed would improve their chances of gaining employment.

Help for those Seeking Employment

19 of the 35 thought that there was insufficient help for young people who were unemployed. Some suggested that more jobs should be created, others that more training opportunities should be made available to alleviate the situation. However, perhaps surprisingly in the light of their own circumstances, 13 of the unemployed group thought that there was enough help.

It would seem that full use was not made of the various local and governmental agencies such as the Careers Office and the Job Centres: 8 of the group had not visited any official agency, although they included some who had personal difficulties at home which made it difficult for them to consider working full-time. Those who had visited such agencies were, perhaps inevitably, critical of the assistance they had received, although 4 did admit that they had sometimes found the agencies helpful.

When asked about their awareness of the various government schemes in operation for alleviating unemployment, and the extent to which they had made use of these schemes, 8 unemployed indicated that they had not considered any of these schemes, and a further 6 claimed never to have heard of them at all. If true, this points to a certain failure to get through to young people just what resources are already available to them.

Nevertheless 12 members of the unemployed group had tried to take advantage of these schemes, and 7 had been accepted.

Attitudes to Unemployment

Half of the unemployed group had not expected to fail in getting a job after leaving school, showing, perhaps, a considerable ignorance of the prevailing employment situation. Their general reactions to being unemployed were mixed: 10 were bored and fed up; 8 didn't like the situation, while 5 complained that they were poor and were short of money. Of the remainder, 5 said they didn't mind and were getting used to the situation.

When asked whether, if they had the opportunity, they would have done anything differently, half said yes. 8 said they would have studied harder for 'O' grades and 3 that they would have stayed on longer at school. Thus, more academic qualifications were seen as the answer to unemployment by 1 in 3 of the group. 13 thought that no-one could really help them with their unemployment difficulties, although 4 mentioned the Careers Office as a possible source of help. Not surprisingly, help in this context was seen as getting an actual job.

On the whole, most of the unemployed thought their main difficulties lay in the general shortage of jobs with too many people chasing them, while others felt that with experience and more qualifications they would have been more successful.

The General Attitude to Work

89% of those interviewed had been looking forward to starting work after leaving school — in the main to earn money or simply to get away from school. The vast majority (82%) had found that their jobs had realised all their expectations.

Initially, 36% had felt apprehensive about starting work, mainly lest they should have difficulty in finding a job, or should choose the wrong job, or one they could not carry out properly. However, these fears proved to have been largely unfounded. Indeed, 68% had found things better than expected, and, on the whole, the young people were well satisfied with their employment.

The group were split more or less evenly on whether or not they would be prepared to work away from home, the boys being much more willing than the girls to do so.

The young people were also asked to indicate how going to work had changed their lives. Three main changes were put

C*

forward: 28% claimed that they now enjoyed greater independence, 24% said that they had more money and 11% said that
they enjoyed work much more than they had enjoyed school.
However 12% of the group did not think that work had altered
their lives in any real way.

CHAPTER 7

INDUCTION, TRAINING AND FURTHER EDUCATION

Induction

The 365 young people who were employed at the time of the interview were asked whether they had received any programme of induction when they started their present job. Induction was explained as "the things you were told about as part of helping you to settle down at work, which were not part of the basic training for your job". Many were clearly unsure as to what constituted induction, and it was often necessary to repeat this definition or to give further explanations.

The great majority of respondents (75%) indicated that they had not undergone any form of induction programme in their present job. Of the 25% who had received some form of induction programme, about half indicated that it had lasted one day or less, and in only a few cases had the programme lasted more than a week. Many of the young people, however, were unable to estimate how many hours in total had been spent in induction.

Those who said they had not had a formal programme of induction were asked who had told them most of the things they wanted to know about on starting work. Most had been helped either by a supervisor, another older worker, or both. The figures also indicated that the girls were more likely to have received help from a supervisor than were the boys, but this was the only significant difference observed.

The vast majority of the whole group (87%) were well satisfied with the type and quantity of information received on entry to work, regardless of whether they had been involved in a formal induction programme. For the 10% who expressed some dissatisfaction, the main problem areas were wages (pay, tax and national insurance), and insufficient details about the actual jobs they would be doing, or the machinery to be used.

Training

365 members of the sample were in employment at the time of the interviews. 27% were undergoing a formal apprenticeship while a further 12% had a period of formal training. 43%, while receiving no formal training, were being trained on the job by a supervisor or other worker. Some 19% (23% of the boys and 14%

of the girls) claimed not to be receiving any training at all in their present job. For those being trained, the general picture that emerged was of satisfaction. Most (77%) thought that their training was well organised and had few suggestions as to how it might be improved.

Opportunities for Training

There were, however, strong sex differences evident in the training opportunities for the group, with the girls being very much disadvantaged. Of the 96 undertaking an apprenticeship, only 7 were girls. 1 boy in 2 was undergoing an apprenticeship. Of those being trained on the job, 67% were girls and only 33% boys. 23% of the girls were receiving no training compared with only 14% of the boys. While 53% of boys had a further education element in their training, usually in connection with an apprenticeship, only 17% of the girls were given such an opportunity. Thus the opportunities for the sexes in terms of training were very different.

When asked whether they would have accepted their present job if there had been no training, 28% said no, basically those who were following apprenticeships. 46% said yes they would, but another 26% made the point that they got no training anyway, and therefore, by implication, had already answered the question positively. As was to be expected, there were again significant sex differences. More boys than girls (39% as against 16%) saw training as an essential requisite in their job, while 33% of girls compared with 19% of boys were already in a job with no training.

Patterns of Training

This section is based on the responses from the 274 members of the group who accepted that they undertook some form of training (some, who were nominally training on the job, claimed not to get any real training). Most of this sub-group (72%) began their training as soon as they joined the firm, but 9% had obviously had a settling-in period of one or two weeks before training began formally, and 6% claimed their training had not begun yet.

The training periods themselves ranged from a few days (4%) to 4 years or longer (30%). Boys, on average, had a 3 year training course while the girls averaged out at 1 year. By contrast, 36% of girls received training for 3 months or less compared with only 6% of boys.

There were 3 main ways in which training was organised. Many (43%) received their training on the job. Another large proportion (24%) had a further education element combined with training on the job. This group tended to be male, only 9 out of 64 being girls. Girls, on the other hand, predominated in another large group (19%) who received a concentrated period of training within the firm, immediately after joining the company. The remainder (12%) took part of their training at a Training Centre combined with training on the job and/or work at college. Thus 1 in 3 of the group had some further education as part of their training, but while half of the boys had such a further education element, only 1 in six of the girls was given a similar opportunity.

Boys were trained largely on the job with or without a college college element. Half of the girls were trained on the job only, and a further third received a concentrated training course run by the company.

61% of the young people in training were trained on an individual basis compared with 28% who were trained on a group basis. The remaining 12% were trained partly in a group and partly on their own.

Qualifications gained

Half of the group indicated that their training would not result in a formal qualification. 27% expected to obtain a City and Guilds Certificate and 4% a National Certificate at either Ordinary or Higher Level. Again, there were strong sex differences. 2 out of 3 boys hoped to get some form of certificate compared with only 1 girl in 4. Only in nursing, secretarial subjects, hairdressing and catering did girls expect to get some form of certification.

Facets of Training

In order to clarify whether those who claimed not to have received any training were perhaps ignoring certain aspects of training, all the employed young people were asked whether they had experienced any of 8 specific ways in which training might have been conducted within the firm, when they first started to work there.

Almost all (85%) had watched experienced workers to see how the job was done, the boys more so than the girls (91% v 80%). Again, most (89%) had received help or had been taught while actually doing the work. 39% had been allowed to practise making things in order to learn the work, and 41% had visited other departments of the firm to see what work was done there.

Some were given literature to read (37%), special talks (31%) or shown films (21%). Very few (8%) had had the opportunity of undertaking refresher courses or retraining courses (which was hardly surprising, since the young people themselves were relative newcomers to the workforce). Boys tended to be given literature and shown films more than girls.

Attitudes to Training

Prior to starting work, 51% of the 298 young people involved had not been told anything about the training they would receive. However 70% had considered training essential. After their experiences of training and work there was a notable shift of opinion. 1 in 3 of those who had previously thought training was unnecessary had changed their minds.

Approximately half of the group were anxious to take more training, generally with a view to earning more money, getting promotion, or keeping up with techniques and specialising. The other half felt they had done enough training and did not really see the need for more.

The group were split over the usefulness of the skills they had learned in their present jobs. Just over half thought these skills would last them all their lives but 43% were less sure and expected they would be required to learn more skills during their working career.

Further Education

42%, less than half of the whole group, had either completed or were currently attending a further education course at the time of the interviews. Approximately 80% of this sub-group indicated that the course undertaken was part of the training for their job, while for the remainder the course was not related to their jobs but was taken purely for interest and usually in the evenings. Significantly more boys than girls were taking further education courses (60% as against 25%).

Many of the young people undertaking further education had begun their courses soon after they started work (43% of the sub-group). Most of the others started not more than 6 months after starting work. Only 1 person in 10 in the further education group began their course after that period. 10 of the group had taken a course before starting work, for example by taking pre-nursing, catering or secretarial courses on a full-time basis as a means of improving their qualifications and experience. There was a significant difference between the times boys and girls started their further education course: boys were more likely to begin shortly after they started work; and the girls to have done a further education course before they started work.

For those going to further education courses, the most common mode of attendance at college was by either day release (57%) or block release (24%). A small proportion were attending evening classes (12% of the sub-group) and a similar proportion were in full-time attendance. Again there were significant differences in the modes by which boys and girls attended their courses. Boys were more likely than girls to be on block release (31% of boys as against 8% of girls), while girls were more likely than boys to be attending full-time courses (27% of girls as against 6% of boys). Day-release attendance was generally similar for both sexes.

The courses followed by the girls were mainly in the areas of secretarial and commercial studies (48%), nursing (17%), and hairdressing (13%). The boys were taking courses in engineering (41%), building trades (17%), and agriculture (6%). Approximately 11% of the further education group were taking SCE courses at 'O' or 'H' level.

The duration of the further education courses normally ranged between 9 months and 4 years. Few courses were for less than 6 months (4%) and even fewer (2%) for more than 4 years. The courses boys were attending were generally of longer duration than the ones girls were taking. 57% of the further education courses taken by boys were for 3 years or more, compared with only 11% of those taken by the girls, whereas 77% of the courses taken by girls lasted for 2 years or less compared with only 38% of those taken by boys.

62% of those involved in an FE course as part of their training (N = 124) indicated that taking the course had been a condition of employment. Again, there were significant differences between boys and girls in this respect: 71% of the boys, compared with 32% of the girls, had been obliged to undertake further education.

The majority (57%) of those not undertaking a further education course (N = 214) had no desire to do so. Of the remainder who did express an interest in further education, 1 in 4 indicated they would like to take 'O' or 'H' grade courses to improve their academic qualifications, while the others were considering more vocationally oriented courses with a view to improving their job situation either through promotion or changing to a better job.

Attitudes to Further Education Courses Undertaken

The general reaction, from those attending FE as part of their training programme, was one of overall satisfaction. Most found it enjoyable and better than they had expected, generally because it was either more interesting or unlike school, and only 18% were positive that they did not enjoy it. Almost all (90%) of those taking further education courses, including those not as part of a training programme, were convinced that the certificate they would gain would be useful for vocational reasons and would enhance their prospects of a better job or promotion. Approximately three-quarters of this sub-group found the subject matter of their college course useful in relation to their work. Most found the course interesting, especially the practical and theoretical aspects, but were less enthusiastic about the general studies component of the course. The majority did not think their course could be improved, but for those who did (1 in 3) changes in course structure or in mode of release were the most common proposals.

Only a few young people (9) indicated they had been obliged to take an FE course against their wishes, generally because the firm required them to take it or because it was the only course available. Otherwise the vast majority (82%) were quite happy with their further education provision.

CHAPTER 8

FUTURE ASPIRATIONS

The young people were asked about their expectations for the future concerning promotion opportunities, earning capabilities and degree of geographical mobility. Girls were asked whether or not they expected to maintain a career after marriage and boys were asked their opinion on working wives. The group were also asked about equal opportunities and how they thought recent legislation had affected them.

Career Prospects

26% of the employed group of 365 members were not optimistic about the potential of their present job and thought it would not lead to anything different in the following 5 years. A further 23% were not sure what, if anything, their job might lead to. However, 24% did expect to have been promoted or to have been given more responsibility within 5 years, and a further 13% expected to be fully qualified tradesmen by then. There were significant differences in the expectations of boys and girls, the boys tending to anticipate more changes than the girls, and more boys than girls (21% v 5%) expecting to be fully qualified. This latter result is partly, if not wholly, a function of the greater number of boys following apprenticeships.

43% of the employed group thought they would be promoted within their present firm, but 13% expected to gain promotion only by moving to a different employer. 37% did not expect promotion at all, with significantly more girls than boys (47% v 28%) in this sub-group. Of the large sub-group (N = 131) who didn't expect to get promotion, many (46%) expected to change jobs occasionally, and 6% frequently, while only 12% expected to stay in their present jobs all their working lives. No sex differences were found within this sub-group.

The majority of the employed group (73%), had not, in fact, discussed their future prospects with anyone within the firm. Of those who had, most had talked with their manager or their direct supervisor. Generally, they had been advised to work hard and to gain further qualifications. Some had been told about promotion and other opportunities within the firm and others had been given advice about college courses.

59% of the employed group did not know what their future

earning capabilities would be. For those who had some idea, the boys expected to average £75 per week by the age of 25 while the girls expected to average only £45 per week — a very substantial difference. These are perhaps realistic figures, given the present higher average earnings of males and females, but they certainly do not point to any strong expectations on the part of girls as regards equal pay in work (no doubt related to type of work obtained).

Mobility

Only 19% of the group had ever considered moving to another part of the United Kingdom, and most of these for better opportunities or for personal reasons. More (30%) had thought of emigrating to countries like Canada, USA, Australia and New Zealand — places where emigration from Scotland has not been uncommon. However, 16 specified somewhere in Europe and 5, perhaps surprisingly, South Africa. Again, better opportunities or family ties or personal preferences were the main reasons specified.

Sex Equality in Work

62% believed that equal opportunities existed for both men and women in finding employment and had not changed this opinion since leaving school and starting work. 87% felt that there should be equal pay for men and women doing the same work. Perhaps predictably, fewer boys than girls agreed with equal pay (79% v 95%).

A considerably different state of affairs emerged, however, when the young people were asked whether equal pay actually happened in practice. Only 31% were convinced that it did. 40% were equally convinced that equal pay did not exist, while 15% qualified their opinion, saying reasonably that equal pay occurred in some occupations but was not universal.

No significant differences between the sexes were found on this question. Thus while the young workforce are largely prepared to accept equal pay as a concept, it is clear that they did not think industry and employers were yet prepared to do so.

The young people were also asked whether they thought the new legislation about equal opportunities (many had to have this explained to them) had made any difference to them personally in the areas of working conditions, training and job opportunities.

Most people (85%) did not think the new laws had made any difference at all. Only some, 5 or 6%, thought that they had. Perhaps surprisingly, since the Sex Discrimination Act was introduced principally to protect women, no significant differences were found between boys and girls regarding the changes produced by the new legislation in the area of work. On the other hand, the timing of the survey was such that it may have been too early for discernible effects to appear.

Marriage and Careers

Girls were asked what effects, if any, they expected marriage to have on their careers, and the boys were asked a different (but similar) question in relation to their wives-to-be. There was little disagreement between the boys and the girls on this issue of the competing roles of women as housewife and worker: in fact, the opinions of the boys generally supported the girls' wishes. 1 in 8 of the girls intended to have a full-time career without marriage. 73% intended to continue working after marriage and 12% intended to be full-time housewives.

Only 15% of the boys felt that their wives should give up work. 37% expected their wives to work full-time, and 17% part-time (the girls were not asked about part-time work). A further 15% were prepared to leave it to the wife to decide, while 4% said it would depend on the situation.

It is clear that girls did not see marriage as an impediment to a working career, and that so far as the young people studied here are concerned, there is likely to be little disagreement as regards the competing roles of woman as housewife and worker.

D

POSTSCRIPT

The work that has been reported in this book was carried out in 1977 at a time when employment prospects for young people leaving school were generally regarded as poor. Today, in 1981, the employment situation is acknowledged to be substantially worse, but most of the data reported in the study is as relevant today as in 1977.

The Munn/Dunning recommendations on a more relevant curriculum and appropriate assessment procedures for the 14-16 year olds, the place of the vocational element in the secondary curriculum, the problem experienced by young people in seeking and finding employment, the provision of suitable guidance to young people through various agencies are all current topics of debate and general discussion in educational and political circles.

This report has provided an opportunity for the young adults in our society to contribute to the debate and to put forward their own opinions on some of the elements of the school/work interface.

APPENDIX: LIST OF TABLES IN THE FULL REPORT*

Chapter numbers refer to those in the full report, and not this summary booklet.

CHAPTER 2: SAMPLE AND DESIGN OF THE PROJECT

2.1 Summary of the interviewing process April-July 1977

2.2 Breakdown of sample x geographical area

2.3 Ability levels of the interviewed and original samples

2.4 Distribution of father's occupational status 1974

2.5 Distribution of young people's occupational aspirations 1974

CHAPTER 4: ATTITUDES TO SCHOOLING

Section 4.1 — Liking for school

4.1.1 How much did subject want to leave school when he/she did?

4.1.2 Reasons for wanting/not wanting to leave school

4.1.3 Whether subject feels he left school at the right time

4.1.4 Reasons why subject feels he should have left school sooner

4.1.5 Reasons why subject feels he should have left school later

4.1.6 Do you like work more or less than school?

4.1.7 Reasons for liking work more than school

4.1.8 Reasons for liking work less than school

Section 4.2 — Advice on employment

4.2.1 Whether school gave subject enough help in preparation for leaving and finding work

4.2.2 Help or preparation for work given by school to those subjects given enough help

---

* Available from the Scottish Council for Research in Education, price on application.

4.2.3   Help or preparation for work given by school to those subjects given insufficient help

4.2.4   What else school could have done for those given insufficient help

Work experience

4.2.5   Whether school arranged for subject to go to firms on work experience schemes

4.2.6   Type of work experience obtained

4.2.7   Whether subject enjoyed work experience scheme

4.2.8   Whether work experience scheme was beneficial to subject

4.2.9   Reasons for finding work experience schemes (a) beneficial (b) not beneficial

4.2.10 Whether those who didn't have opportunity to do a work experience scheme would have liked to do so

4.2.11 Reasons why subjects would like to have gone on a work experience scheme

4.2.12 Reasons why subjects did not want to go on a work experience scheme

Technical College visits

4.2.13 Whether school arranged for subject to visit a Technical College

4.2.14 Length of visit to Technical College

4.2.15 Whether visit to Technical College was interesting

4.2.16 Reasons for finding Technical College visit (a) interesting (b) not interesting

4.2.17 Whether those who didn't have the opportunity to visit a Technical College would have liked to do so

Link courses

4.2.18 Whether school arranged for subject to take a course at Technical College

4.2.19 Types of courses taken at Technical College

4.2.20 Length of Technical College course

4.2.21 Whether subject found Technical College course beneficial

CHAPTER 5: ADVICE ON EMPLOYMENT

Section 5.1 —   Sources of guidance before leaving school

CHAPTER 6: SEEKING EMPLOYMENT

Section 6.1 — **Number and type of jobs sought**

6.1.1 Whether subject started looking for jobs before leaving school

6.1.2 Length of time before leaving school subject started looking for employment

6.1.3 Length of time after leaving school that subject started looking for work

6.1.4 Length of time taken to find work

6.1.5 Number of jobs applied for before getting a job

6.1.6 Skill-level of first job accepted x sex

6.1.7 Occupational area of job first accepted x sex

6.1.8 Selection procedure undergone for first job accepted x sex

6.1.9 Skill-levels of other recorded job applications x sex

6.1.10 Occupational areas of additional jobs applied for x sex

6.1.11 Results of other job applications

6.1.12 Selection procedure undergone for other job applications x sex

Section 6.2 — **Difficulties encountered in seeking umployment**

6.2.1 Number of jobs offered to subjects

6.2.2 Was subject offered first job applied for?

6.2.3 Reasons for not accepting job offered

6.2.4 Reason for choosing job accepted when choice available

6.2.5 Young peoples' opinions on finding a job

6.2.6 Reasons for finding getting a job difficult

6.2.7 Reasons for finding getting a job easy

Section 6.3 — **Previous job history**

6.3.1 Period of time unemployed immediately after leaving school

6.3.2 Number of jobs subjects had had since leaving school

6.3.3 Skill-levels of previous jobs held by subjects

6.3.4 Previous jobs by occupational area

Section 6.6 — Attitudes to work generally

CHAPTER 7: INDUCTION AND TRAINING

Section 7.1 — Induction

Section 7.2 — The training process

7.2.2	Length of training schemes in previous jobs
7.2.3	Whether there was any FE associated with training in previous jobs
7.2.4	Whether subject attended this FE component
7.2.5	Whether subject was told everything he wanted to know
7.2.6	What subject was not told about
7.2.7	Type of training subject is receiving in present job
7.2.8	Whether subject is receiving part-time FE as part of training
7.2.9	Whether subject would have accepted the present job if there had been no training
7.2.10	Reasons for wanting/not wanting training
7.2.11	When training began
7.2.12	How long training period lasted
7.2.13	What subjects thought the length of training should be
7.2.14	How training was organised
7.2.15	Whether subjects were trained in a group or on their own
7.2.16	Qualifications, if any, that training led to
7.2.17	Numbers (percentages) experiencing specific facets of training
7.2.18	Sex differences in facets of training
7.2.19	What is good about the training in subjects' firms
7.2.20	What is bad about the training in subjects' firms
7.2.21	What changes subjects would like to see made in their training
7.2.22	Why subjects wanted these changes to be made
7.2.23	What subjects were told about training before starting work
7.2.24	Whether subjects felt training was necessary before they started work
7.2.25	How subjects felt about training now
7.2.26	Whether subjects would like to do any more training
7.2.27	Reasons why subjects want to take additional training
7.2.28	Reasons for subjects not wishing to do any more training

7.2.29   Whether subjects thought their present training would help them in other jobs

7.2.30   What subjects expect of the skills learnt in present jobs

Section 7.3 —   Further education undertaken

7.3.1   Whether subject is or will be taking any FE courses

7.3.2   Whether those taking FE or intending to take FE do so as part of their training

7.3.3   When subjects started FE course x sex

7.3.4   Method of attendance at FE course x sex

7.3.5   Type of FE course being attended x sex

7.3.6   How long did the course last

7.3.7   Would subject have been accepted for present job without doing an FE course

7.3.8   Whether subject asked anyone about what he/she would do at college

7.3.9   What subject enquired about

7.3.10   Did subject find advice in college helpful

7.3.11   Whether those not taking any FE courses would like to do so

7.3.12   Which courses would subjects like to take

7.3.13   Reasons for wishing to take a particular FE course

7.3.14   Why subjects not taking desired FE course

7.3.15   Reason why subjects have no wish to take an FE course

Section 7.4 —   Reactions to further education courses undertaken

7.4.1   Whether subject likes going to Technical College

7.4.2   Before starting course what subject expected course to be like

7.4.3   Whether course is better or worse than subject expected

7.4.4   In which ways course was different from what subject expected

7.4.5   Does subject think certificate gained from the course will prove useful

7.4.6   Reasons why certificate will be useful
7.4.7   Does subject find what is learned at college useful
7.4.8   Ways in which subject finds college course useful/not useful
7.4.9   Opinions of subjects on various aspects of the course taken
7.4.10 Reasons for no aspect of the course being endorsed
7.4.11 Could college course be improved
7.4.12 In which ways could the course have been improved
7.4.13 Whether subject wanted to do the course he was put on
7.4.14 Reason for subject not wanting to do the course he/she was put on
7.4.15 Reason why subject was put on this course

CHAPTER 8: FUTURE ASPIRATIONS

8.1   What subject thinks his present job will lead to in 5 years x sex
8.2   Young person's expectations as regards promotion
8.3   Job expectations of those who don't expect promotion
8.4   How much subject expects to be earning per week by age 25 x sex
8.5   Whether subject has ever discussed his future with anyone at work
8.6   What advice for the future did the people at work give subject
8.7   Has subject considered moving to another part of the country
8.8   To which area of the country subject thought of moving
8.9   Reason why subject has thought of moving
8.10 Has subject thought of emigrating
8.11 To which country has subject thought of emigrating
8.12 Reason why subject has thought of emigrating
8.13 Attitudes to woman's career after marriage x sex

8.14   Whether, before leaving school, subject felt
        he/she had equal opportunities with girls or boys
        respectively of the same age in finding a job
8.15   How does subject feel about equal opportunities
        now
8.16   Does subject think there should be equal pay for
        men and women doing the same kind of job
8.17   Does subject think that equal pay happens in
        practice
8.18   Does subject feel new laws about equal oppor-
        tunities have made much difference to him/her